ROHAN CANDAPPA

UNIVERSITY CHALLENGED

EBURY PRESS

First published by Ebury Press in Great Britain in 2003

1 3 5 7 9 10 8 6 4 2

Ebury Press
Random House · 20 Vauxhall Bridge Road · London SW1V 2SA

Random House Australia Pty Limited
20 Alfred Street · Milsons Point · Sydney · New South Wales 2061 · Australia

Random House New Zealand Limited
18 Poland Road · Glenfield · Auckland 10 · New Zealand

Random House (Pty) Limited
Endulini · 5A Jubilee Road · Parktown 2193 · South Africa

The Random House Group Limited Reg. No. 954009

www.randomhouse.co.uk

Papers used by Ebury Press are natural, recyclable products
made from wood grown in sustainable forests.

A CIP catalogue record for this book is available from the British Library.

ISBN 0091886643

Text design by Lovelock & Co.
Cover design by Two Associates

Printed and bound in Denmark by
Nørhaven Paperback, Viborg

For Pauline and Martin and Emily. And Bob (of the perfectly formed forearms) and the semi-legendary Derb. And Vicky. And for Sir Thomas Lambchop, the party at Swampside where we flooded the patio, and for the missing exhaust pipe of Nipper's Ducati. And for Lindsey.

And with sincere apologies to Dr Sophie Bowlby.

Be afraid, Be very afraid

Going to university can be a daunting affair. There are so many new experiences to try, so many responsibilities to handle and so many parent-shocking debts to be accumulated. What you really need to help you through it all is a best friend who'll show you the ropes, hold your hand when it needs holding and make sure you get to your lectures on time.

This book, unfortunately, isn't that friend. This book, even more unfortunately, is more akin to the kind of mate who doesn't get up until half past two, nicks your food from the fridge and, when you're both well wasted at some awful party you've gate-crashed, convinces you that Baileys, cider and Worcestershire sauce is a real cocktail.

Frankly, if you have even the slightest ambition to emerge from your time in 'higher' education with any kind of qualification whatsoever, it's best that you stop reading now. If, however, you insist on perusing the 'wisdom' contained within this highly disreputable tome, then please note that the author accepts no responsibility for the fact that you'll get a crap qualification, that your parents will disown you, that your subsequent career will go nowhere and, in all probability, your future marriage will end in an acrimonious divorce.

But all that lies way off in the future. So let's talk about Freshers' Week.

Freshers' Week

Parental advice

Before you go to university your parents will give you lots of advice. Now I believe that it's very important that while at university you always remember that advice. And should you ever find yourself following any of it, quickly do the opposite.

Your time at university
– an analogy for freshers

Don't think of it as time spent studying, think of it as a Voyage Of Discovery. A voyage on which hearty new-found companions will make your acquaintance ready and able to accompany you on the Journey Of Life. A journey at whose end a whole new world of possibilities awaits you.

In fact, in many ways, being at university is just like a trip on the *Titanic*. And look how well that turned out.

What to say to friends from home who got into other universities

The key point here is to over-exaggerate just how great a time you're having, how stonking the nightlife is, and how you've hooked up with a gang of new mates who it feels like you've known all your life.

This gives you the best chance of making your old friends feel really bad about the place they got into.

Why halls of residence are often bleak, soulless, depressing places

It's a cunning ploy by the government to put you off a life of crime. As in, should you decide to turn to lawlessness this is the kind of accommodation that awaits you.

The other reason why halls of residence are often bleak, soulless, depressing places

It's a lot cheaper that way.

Posters

Many halls of residence explicitly ban the use of
Sellotape or BluTack for sticking up posters in your
room because of the damage these adhesives do to
the walls. However, very few halls of residence have
any instructions banning the use of glue or nails.

Act accordingly.

The main difference between school and university

The main difference is to do with responsibility. At school the key educational responsibility is for teachers to teach you. At university the key educational responsibility is for you to learn. Unfortunately most students don't learn this until long after they've left. I tell you this in the vain hope that it might galvanise you into taking responsibility for expanding your mind. But in the full knowledge that you won't. After all, you are a student.

Lazy sod.

Alarm clocks

It is vital that you take an alarm clock to university. This is not so that you can wake up in time for lectures or exams. This is so that you don't miss lunch.

Brightening up your room

Plants are a great way to make an otherwise uninviting environment homely. Unfortunately, buying plants from shops or garden centres can be very expensive. Luckily, most towns and cities have plenty of well-stocked municipal parks with pleasingly low fences.

Joining clubs and societies at Freshers' Fair

At Freshers' Fair you will encounter more activities, sports and obscure-sounding groups than you ever knew existed. And they'll all try to convince you that by joining them your time at university will be transformed into one non-stop round of excitement, achievement and enjoyment.

Unfortunately this isn't true.

But if you do join them you'll have the chance to encounter and observe the people who run the societies. This is important because these are the same people who will, in later life, end up running 'society' as a whole.

Which kind of explains why society is such a well-meaning but essentially amateurish affair.

The 'efficient use of your time' speech

At some point early on in your university career someone in authority will give you the speech about how it's up to you to make 'efficient use of your time'.

In my opinion the most 'efficient use of your time' would be to ignore the speech.

The two most important things to locate during Freshers' Week

Conventional wisdom would have it that the two most important things to find during Freshers' Week are your hall of residence and the library.

In fact, the two most important things to locate are the whereabouts of the nearest kettle to your room and the nearest toaster. Get this sorted and the rest of the week will probably take care of itself. Indeed, many would argue that throughout your entire university career knowledge of the whereabouts of the nearest kettle and toaster is all you really need to survive.

Homesickness

If you're feeling homesick it's important you realise that you're the only person who's ever felt like this, you don't fit in, everyone else is having a great time, you can't cope, it's not ever going to get any better and you're just one great big loser.

Alternatively, everyone feels homesick from time to time, everyone else isn't having a better time (they're probably just better at disguising their worries), how to cope with it all is something you can and will learn in time, and things will get better especially if you stay sober enough to speak.

Mind you, you might still be a loser. But, hey, I can't help you with everything.

The real reason why your parents were so keen that you further your education by going to university

They wanted you out of the house.

The cuddly toy rule

First-year students of the female variety are often tempted to take a cuddly toy from home. The role of said cuddly toy is to keep them company in their room and to, metaphorically speaking, hold at bay the large and confusing world that is university.

On the whole this is inadvisable. That's because it reveals far too much about the fragile state of your confidence. What may come across as charming, childlike naivety when you were packing your stuff at home to head off universitywards is rarely seen in the same light by your fellow students.

However, if you must take a cuddly toy be sure to be well versed in the Universal University Cuddly Toy Rule:

1. One cuddly toy is OK for your first term if:
   a. It is kept discreetly displayed by your bed.
   b. It is never cuddled when in the company of other students.

c. You never reveal how close you are to
    tears when male student 'friends'
    play with it in a cavalier fashion, or
    decide to take it out on a bar crawl.

2. Two cuddly toys is pushing it a bit, but you
    might just get away with it if you strictly adhere
    to the advice outlined above and ensure that one
    of the cuddly toys is in some way 'ironic'.

3. Three cuddly toys is a definite no-no. Frankly,
    turn up at university with three cuddly toys and
    you might as well hang a sign around your neck
    that reads 'I am sad'. You should also prepare
    yourself for three years of social disappointment,
    eventual marriage to a terribly dull man called
    Malcolm, and no real experience of orgasm until
    you flee the marital home in your mid thirties
    and take solace in the delights of the love that
    dare not speak its name with a strong-wristed
    lady from Munich named Gerta.

Game over

There is, of course, an equally dubious male equivalent of the female student cuddly toy thing. I speak of the supposed delights of electronic gamery. And here's why.

To start with, one of the fundamental appeals of computer games is that they provide a world of excitement, adventure and conflict in which – and this is key – you ultimately have no responsibility for anything you do or how badly you behave. But isn't that why you came to university?

Frankly, if you haven't figured out that being a student is the only time in your life when you can act like you are in a computer game, then, metaphorically speaking, you're well stuck in Training Mode.

The second reason to put away all computer games at university is to do with girls. Girls don't really get the computer game thing. To them a bloke who spends hours at a time glued to a screen seems as absurd as if they themselves still spent whole afternoons playing with Barbie dolls. And it doesn't matter how macho the game is that you're playing. There isn't a girl in the land who sits around supping a Babycham and Baileys of an evening, eyeing up the talent and going, 'Phwoar, look at him, I bet he's on Level Six!'

So, chaps, if you want to have even the remotest chance of getting laid, then please lay down the controls of your console, or condemn yourself to a succession of solitary nights in your room, playing with your own joystick.

Gap kids

No, I'm not talking about the clothes store. I'm talking about students who've spent a year between school and university out in the big wide world.

If you are one of these, the course of action to create the maximum irritation is clear. Affect an air of condescending maturity and regale all those around you with endless tales of the fabulous places you've been and crazy things you got up to.

If you aren't one of these 'seasoned travellers' but have to endure their giga-boring Y.H.T.B.T.* stories, your best response is to try a bit of your own travelling whenever one of these dullards turns up.

Which isn't to say that travel doesn't broaden the mind, because it does. It's just that formalising and containing the possibilities that are inherent within cutting loose and seeing where the spirit takes you into something as ultimately conservative and conformist as a Gap Year is deeply suspect.

What I'm driving at is this. Why settle for a Gap Year when you could have a Gap Life?

* You Had To Be There

Hall food

It's like Jamie Oliver had never been born. (Or had decided to be a chiropodist.)

Corridor parties

An integral part of student life for anyone living in a hall of residence are parties that actually take place in the corridor. They work for a variety of reasons. For a start a corridor is a narrow space, so they always seem crowded. Also, because the space is confined there are ample opportunities to inadvertently brush against, or lean into, someone you fancy. But more important than all this is the fact that the party is in a public place – which means that you have the added bonus of letting passers-by know that you're having a great time, and they're not.

Freshers' Week friends

It is a well-established university phenomenon that during Freshers' Week you will meet people who miraculously seem to be the closest, best and truest friends that you have ever had in your life. You will sally forth, side by side, into each new day and each new night eager to experience all that university has to offer. Every passing second will cement a bond that you just know will last a lifetime.

Unfortunately, by Week Three you will realise that you have absolutely nothing in common with them and you will find that you spend the rest of the term, and indeed the rest of your time at university, desperately trying to avoid them.

(Equally unfortunately, ten years after you graduate, when against your better judgement you decide to attend a university reunion, they will be the very person that you'll be seated next to.)

Beyond Freshers' Week

A brief note on the structure of the rest of this book

What lies ahead of you at university is an unholy mess barely contained within the flimsiest of structures. And it's a state of affairs that I've tried to replicate in this book. So start at any page, head in any direction, and the advice that you find will be just as irrelevant, crap and devoid of any practical use.

Which makes it just like the textbooks that you've so recently shelled out for. Only it's a lot cheaper.

The age-old boyfriend/girlfriend back at home quandary

Hey, look, I know you really love them. It's just that as time goes on and your life at university really gets going you will inevitably start to feel that what you have isn't as appealing as what you could have.

Then your mind starts to wander along the path that goes, 'Of course I love you but...' And it's that single word 'but' that reveals the truth.

Well, university is all about seizing the opportunities that life has to offer. And what's the point of going to the seaside if you're not going to go in for a swim? So the kindest thing to do is to end the relationship back at home quickly and cleanly. The cleaner the break, the easier it will be for both of you to move on.

And the sooner you end it, the sooner you can get back to pursuing that person you snogged during Freshers' Week without feeling guilty.

How to sensitively dump your girlfriend/boyfriend back at home

You can't go wrong with a text message.

The first trip back home

In your parents' eyes you left home as a child. But you return as... what? Of course they will expect you to have changed, but it's the precise nature of that change that will inevitably fill them with trepidation.

For maximum impact, even if you are pretty much the same person that went away, go overboard on imaginary alterations. Change your clothes, change your hair, change your speech patterns, change what you eat, change how much you drink, change what you think and, the real icing on the cake, change your sexuality.

Now if you can't get some fun out of a scenario like that, then you're not really trying.

Ten things to do to pass the time during a lecture

1. Sleep.
2. Look out of the window.
3. Look in through the window and realise you should be inside. Taking notes.
4. Send text messages to a friend.
5. Send text messages to a friend sleeping in the same lecture.
6. Flirt with another student.
7. Flirt with the lecturer.
8. Obsess about whether a fellow student had meant what they said about their feelings for you last night when you were both quite drunk.
9. Pretend to take notes.
10. Pretend to take drugs.

The importance of music to the modern university student

As a university student you will find that it is vital you have your own personal soundtrack. Outlined below are the five types of music you should be au fait with in order to fully establish your student credentials.

1. A favourite band/singer

All students must have a favourite band or singer. You should buy their CDs the day they're released and know all the words within a week. Having a favourite band/singer will give you a fairly risk-free topic of conversation when meeting new people. And indeed it could be argued that asking someone what kind of music they like is the natural next step on from the Holy Trinity of questions all university students employ when encountering someone new. (The Holy Trinity being, 'Where are you from? What are you studying? Where are you staying?') Should the person you're talking to like the same band/singer that you do then it's only a question of time before you move on to Question Five. (Question Five being 'Do you fancy a shag?')

2. The floor filler
This is a song/track that comes on at a university disco/gig/party and will always get you up from your seat and dancing. Usually badly.

3. The Drunken Singalong Song or D.S.S.
Alcohol really is a most remarkable substance. Imbibe enough of the stuff and it can convince even the most tone deaf, tune murdering among you that you can sing. And that you should share your vocal talents with those unfortunates around you. The D.S.S. is the song that lets you let rip. Popular D.S.Ss have included 'Don't Look Back In Anger' by Oasis, 'Angels' by Robbie Williams and the all-time favourite 'Dancing Queen' by ABBA. The approved technique for delivering a D.S.S. involves going to a party, failing to get off with the person you fancy, drinking too much, then

standing in the middle of the room, throwing your arms around your mate, swaying like a halibut in a hurricane, and screeching at full volume in your compadre's ear the words of your chosen ditty in a way that conveys a wry disappointment with the ironies of life, a mutual bond of true affection and a 'fuck 'em all' to the losers who turned the pair of you down.

Then you go outside and throw up in a bush.

4. The obscurity
It is also worthwhile knowing the name of some impossible-to-track-down obscurity, be it band or song, whose genius you can proclaim in order to impress fellow students. This information should always be imparted with just a hint of condescending disdain, e.g. 'You mean you haven't heard the Cannibal Ferox remix?'

5. W.S.M.
As a student it is vital that you always have about your room some W.S.M. This, in case you don't

know, stands for Wrist Slashing Music. That's the music that you play very loud, very late at night whenever your love life has gone wrong. Or not even started yet. Or you're depressed about work. Or you feel totally out of place. Or you miss home. Or you hate the way you look.

Wrist Slashing Music provides the vital soundtrack to the hours you spend curled up on your bed, clinging to your pillow, wallowing in self-pity. Without it your situation could, unjustly, be seen as just a little bit pathetic. With it your wallowing becomes altogether more poetic, meaningful and ever so slightly cinematic.

Good W.S.M. includes much of the output of Coldplay, Radiohead, Eva Cassidy and the hard-to-track-down cult classic 'S Club Juniors Sing Joy Division'.

Why it's always good to have a little sob when your parents drop you off at the start of term

It makes it so much easier to get money out of them later on.

The recommended daily intake of alcohol units. And how to get round it

One unit of alcohol is generally equated with half a pint of normal strength beer, a small glass of wine, or a single measure of spirits. The recommended daily intake for women is 2-3 units. The recommended daily intake for men is 3-4 units.

For the average student this presents a problem.

But there is a way round it. All you need do is invoke the L.A.D.D.I. This is the Lifetime Average Daily Drinking Index. This allows your daily consumption of alcohol to be averaged out over your lifetime.

So when you take into account that you probably didn't drink much alcohol as a small- to medium-sized child, and probably won't be allowed to drink much later on in life when your kidneys fail, then you can drink as much as you like now.

A few thoughts on the university wispy beard phenomenon

Invariably the grower of the wispy beard thinks it makes him look older. Unfortunately, viewers of those who grow wispy beards tend to think, 'Gosh, he must look really young because he's grown a wispy beard to try and make himself look older.'

It's rather like those ageing male rock stars who always wear hats hoping that no-one will figure out that they're really going bald.

Please turn over the corner of this page in case one of your parents picks up this book while visiting you.

Sex is not something to be entered into lightly. Though there will no doubt be many temptations presented to you during your time at university it is best not to give yourself to another until you are in a stable and loving relationship. All things considered, your wisest course of action is to wait until you and your partner are married.

The university student's guide to kissing

Kissing at university is a far more complex business than it ever was at school. A brief guide follows.

The art student kiss

This kiss is best executed with the eyes tightly shut and all attention focused on both the sensations of the kiss and how to describe it should one ever have to write down what the kiss was like in, for example, a diary, a letter to your best friend, or an essay entitled 'The Contrasting Significance Of The Kiss In The Late Novels Of Thomas Hardy And Mid 1990s Photo Love Stories From *Sugar* Magazine'. The kiss should hint at intelligence, creativity and humour. And at parents who have well-paid, exciting-sounding but essentially meaningless jobs in the media.

The science student kiss

This kiss should only be executed under controlled conditions. Prior to the kiss it is vital that the kisser considers the hypothesis that's being tested and sets definable parameters for the kiss. Possible hypotheses include: does the kissee fancy me?, does the kissee fancy a shag?, or has the kissee been eating left-over and slightly crusty macaroni cheese lately? The results should be assiduously noted down and cross-referenced against earlier kisses to see if any patterns or trends emerge. Plotting the kiss on an X-Y graph, where Y represents Kiss Duration and X represents Arousal is also advisable.

The social science kiss
A well-meaning but ultimately confused kiss that's of little or no use in the world outside university.

The fresher's kiss
The fresher's kiss is made up of equal measures of insecurity and over-confidence. Thoughts that occur during a fresher's kiss include:

'Is this right?' 'Is he/she right?' 'How far should I go?' 'How far will I get?' 'I hope (enter name of partner at home here) never finds out.' 'Oh my God, I'm in love! At last! This feels so good, so right, I know I've only just met him yesterday but we spent the whole night drinking coffee and just talking about everything and it was so deep and he was so funny, and I know it sounds corny but when I spotted him in the queue for lunch my heart actually leapt, I knew choosing this university was right and the thing I can't get over is that he's so good-looking, I mean, it's not as if acne lasts for ever...'

and

'I hope I put the condom on right.'

The second-year kiss

The second-year kiss is a confident, knowing kiss. It is a kiss that has found a place to call its own. It has jettisoned the uncertainties of fresherdom and is as yet untroubled by the looming realities of the Final Year. Lips, tongues and playful teeth are all employed in the second-year kiss. And passion is tempered by tenderness.

The final-year kiss

Tenderness? My arse! The final-year kiss reveals just what a grubby business all this mouth-to-mouth canoodling really is. All pretence at love is replaced by a burgeoning sense of foreboding. Outwardly confident and seemingly masterful though the final-year kiss appears, it takes but the briefest bout of lip-lockery to reveal that at its core is a tongue frantically trying to dig its way out of a hole. This isn't passion, this is panic. The final-year kiss is coarse, dribbly and a mere prelude to a morning after full of ugly recriminations and unanswered text messages.

The kiss of the tutor

All you really need to know is you won't be the first. Or the last. And the delicious illicitness of it aside, it won't actually be much good. (What's more, when you finally go back years after you've graduated they won't remember who you are, and you won't remember what you saw in them in the first place.)

The three most important uses of the university library

Sleeping.
Flirting.
Hiding.

A shocking truth about textbooks

Just buying the books isn't enough. You actually have to open and read them.

A point to keep in mind when taking part in all manner of student discussions

Never let lack of knowledge on a particular subject prevent you from joining in, or even dominating, the discussion.

Charity shop chic

One way of saving money while at university is to buy your clothes from charity shops. Rumour has it that with just a careful sorting and selection process you can put together a look that is both fashionable and inexpensive. Unfortunately, rumour can be a right lying bastard at times. The truth is you're much more likely to end up in dodgy-coloured clothes that don't fit particularly well and are just ever so slightly whiffy.

To misquote Mark Twain

At university it is vitally important that you never let lectures interfere with your education.

The star lecturer myth

Some of you will have been attracted to choose a particular course on account of the presence of a 'star' lecturer. No doubt the university prospectus informed you that Professor Big Bollocks plays a key part in the teaching of said course.

Unfortunately, the prospectus lied.

The problem with a star lecturer is that they are a star. As such they are far too valuable a resource for the university to have them waste any of their precious time on anything so unimportant as teaching.

And that's why when you got your course reading list, top of the items that you had to buy was Professor Big Bollocks' latest book. Because the book is the closest you're going to get to an insight into their mind.

What's more, their ten-years-out-of-date picture on the back cover gives you an outside chance of recognising the elusive bastard in the unlikely event of you ever coming across them in the department.

Uni

Calling university 'uni' is an affectation. So don't do it. After all, you don't refer to your time at school as 'scho'. And when you eventually leave university it's very unlikely that you'll ever refer to your employment as your 'jo'. Therefore, unless you want to be thought of by your fellow students as a bit of a 'wan', please don't call university 'uni'.

Kebabs

One of the great joys of university is that it will introduce you to philosophies of life that you previously had no idea existed. Prime amongst these is the study of the kebab in contemporary Western society.

Indeed, some argue that the humble kebab is a fitting metaphor for university. For example, the pitta bread is the empty shell that is the student, the meat is the academic education that is loaded into the student, the salady bits are the social skills that the student accrues by living away from home, and the chilli sauce is the promise of debauchery that spices up the whole university experience.

The fact that a kebab usually falls apart into an incoherent mess of soggy pitta, doner shavings and limp lettuce, leaving dribbles of chilli sauce down the front of your clothes and a feeling of nausea in the pit of your stomach, is also a fair indication of what awaits you after you graduate.

Other aspects of the kebab you may usefully study at university

Kebabology How to define an individual's true nature by the type of kebab they favour.

Kebabrobics How to up your fitness level with the aid of a large, fully loaded kebab.

Kebabraphobia A study of the sad and irrational fear some students have of the kebab.

Kebabphilia Let's just say an extreme 'over-fondness' of the kebab.

Kebab Shui The ancient Chinese art of rearranging the contents of the kebab in order to improve your life.

Feminist Kebab Theory A detailed sociological analysis based on the revelation that the insertion of the whole chilli into the waiting doner is nothing but the symbolic recreation of the penetration of the supposedly 'compliant' female by the 'dominant' male and hence a reassertion of oppressive, paternalistic power structures.

(N.B. This is also thought to explain why the kebab is, generally speaking, a male food. And a food they're only 'man' enough to eat after a bellyful of lager. In the United States, of course, the whole F.K.T. paradigm was pushed further by a group of radical, lesbian, feminist students who marched on Bill Clinton's White House under a banner provocatively claiming 'Ain't No Chilli In My Kebab!')

Should you 'make' notes or 'take' notes during a lecture?

'Making' notes involves sitting in a lecture and writing down what you hazard a guess at being the important stuff that the lecturer is banging on about. 'Taking' notes involves waiting until the lecture is over, then distracting a fellow student with some cunning ploy and nicking the notes they have made. Accordingly, for the canny student it is far better to 'take' notes than it is to 'make' notes.

Heave ho!

University is also the ideal place to investigate the full gamut of possibilities contained within different styles of puking. These include:

The Dribble
The Single Heave
The Retch
The Epicentre And Aftershocks
The Simmer
The Bubbling Soup
The New Shoes
The Fist
The Fist And Twist
The Anatomy Lesson

and the truly disgusting

F.K.H. – French Kiss Heave

No student can think of themselves as having truly graduated until they've crossed off at least four of the methodologies listed above.

Three reasons why baked beans are the true cornerstones of university life

1. They're cheap.
2. They're nutritious.
3. They encourage farting.

Now what more could a student possibly want from a food?

Tutorial bingo

This is a great way to pass the time in group tutorials. Before the tutorial starts, choose a group of words. It could be colours, or animals, or song titles by a particular artist. Then each participant scores a point each time they manage to work one of these words into the discussion in the tutorial.

The late sleeper's guide to what happens in the mornings

Breakfast, lectures, crap TV and birds singing. (So you're not really missing much.)

How to deal with being in love with someone who doesn't love you

Unfortunately this is all too common a scenario in the emotional hotbed of university life. Luckily, there is a relatively easy solution. First go out for the evening with the object of your devotion and a group of your mutual mates. Over the course of the night nervously drink more than you usually do. Then, as everyone heads home, inveigle an invitation to said loved one's room for a 'chat'. Talk about anything but the real subject on your mind. All the time remember to keep drinking. Finally, as your loved one's eyes start to droop, realise that it's now or never, drunkenly pour forth your heart, leap on top of them and try to kiss them.

That should do the trick.

A thought to bare in mind as you head home for the holidays

Going to university gives you the right to explain things to your parents.

The H.G.I.

Decades of research in universities the length and
breadth of the country has proven the veracity of
the Hangover Grease Index. This axiom states that
the bigger the hangover a student is suffering, the
greasier the fry-up they should ingest to counter it.

Indeed, should you find yourself in the far from
tender clutches of The Hangover From Hell, skip
the culinary fripperies of the egg, bacon and
sausage altogether and go straight for the packet
of lard.

The catchphrase sweepstake

This is another fine way to make your invariably dull lectures go faster. Prior to the lecture get together with a group of fellow students and each put up a small monetary stake. Then write down on a piece of paper how long each of you think it will be before the lecturer you're about to be lectured by uses his favourite word or phrase. Appoint a non-betting student as official timekeeper and instruct them to start timing from the moment the lecture begins. Whoever's predicted time is closest to the actual utterance of the selected word or catchphrase wins the money.

Staying up all night, drinking coffee and talking about life, the universe and everything

This is really important student stuff. And though, on the face of it, the scope, range and intensity of the discussions are what really matters, they're not. What really matters is that you're not the first to go to bed. That's because what's really going on here is the establishment of a hierarchy of studentness. And he or she who, bleary-eyed, admits tiredness and throws in the towel first, has definitely just been relegated from the Premier League.

Seven key concepts with which all students must be au fait

1. Existentialism.
2. Post modernism.
3. Apathy.
4. Angst.
5. Hedonism.
6. Irony.
7. Timmy Mallett.

A few words of reassurance about the beautiful people

Every university has them. Students who seem somehow blessed. They're better looking, better dressed, and seem to be having a far better time than anyone else. They get invited to all the best parties, never seem to be weighed down with worries about workloads, and manage to be in gloriously passionate relationships with the most desirable of partners.

Every sight of them just reminds you what a drab nonentity of a student you really are.

However, before you put yourself down too much you can console yourself with this thought: for the beautiful people university is as good as it gets. And their particular Golden Age will wither in the harsh realities of the outside world. So, seen in the context of a lifetime, peaking while at university is most definitely a case of metaphorical premature ejaculation. Oh yes, they may well be having loads of fun now, but believe me, they'll be washing their sheets for a long time afterwards.

An old saying. Extended

Those who can – do. Those who can't – teach.
Those who can't teach – become lecturers at
university, have tenure and can't be fired.

Why you should try and avoid contact
with mature students

It's because they came to university to study. It's a
reprehensible attitude that may well rub off. So
your best course is to steer well clear of them.

A short treatise on the 42 different types of sex available to students

OK, so you may well have had sex before you got to university, but once at university a whole smorgasbord of possibilities opens up for you. In order to guide you through this potential minefield, I will point out some of the main options available:

The Quickie Any sex you can complete during an ad break on TV.

The Quick Quickie Any sex you can complete during an advert on TV.

The Slowie Any sexual encounter that takes longer than half an hour.

The Slow Slowie Any sexual encounter that takes longer than half a term.

The Slow, Slow, Quick, Quick, Slowie An advanced sexual shenanigan usually the preserve of the Ballroom Dancing Society and involving lots of sequins.

The Knee Trembler A type of Quickie, often against a wall, or in a car seat.

The Elbow Trembler Masturbation.

The Knee And Elbow Trembler A sexual encounter with someone who's very nervous or suffering from Parkinson's.

The Missionary Position Sex with the male student on top and the female student on a gap year in Africa.

The Submissionary Position Sex with the female student on top and the male student on all fours crawling around the room licking clean his partner's shoes.

The BJ A blow job.

The BLT A type of sandwich. (You really should get out more.)

Vestiality A sordid and grubby perversion involving fornication with someone who insists on wearing a vest.

Break-Up Sex An either angry or tender encounter indulged in as the final farewell act of intimacy after you've told someone you're leaving them.

Make-Up Sex Truly blissful love-making that follows the realisation that you were wrong to break up in the first place.

Shake-Up Sex Sex with someone who isn't your partner, which you indulge in because in your warped mind you rationalise (with impeccable student logic) it will prove to your partner that other people find you desirable, so spur them on to realise what a good thing they've got in you, and hence actually strengthen your relationship.

Cake-Up Sex Sex involving chocolate eclairs and ring doughnuts.

Doggy Style A position that replicates the mating stance of hounds.

Advanced Doggy Style A position strictly for the uninhibited that takes doggy style one step further by having you and your partner assume the position in full view next to a park bench, or on the pavement next to a bus queue.

96 Similar to the well-known 69 but with the positions reversed.

Ex Sex Sex that you know you'll regret in the morning with someone that you used to be involved with.

Access All Areas An advanced, no-holds-barred encounter that's really best saved until you've left university, found yourself trapped in a loveless marriage and embarked on a sordid affair that will ultimately end in tears.

Excess All Areas Similar to the last entry, but involving copious amounts of drink, drugs or that other great inhibition loosener – love.

Brushing The Suede Don't ask.

A Cup A Soup Any kind of sex that seems a good idea at the start but halfway through you realise is totally gross.

A Bactrian Any session that involves making love twice in quick succession.

Rumpy Pumpy Anal sex.

Slumpy Pumpy Sex with someone who just lies there.

Grumpy Pumpy Sex with someone who just lies there, in a bad mood.

Dumpy Pumpy A cruel variation on Break-Up Sex where you make love first, then tell your partner that you're leaving them.

A Maradona A hand job.

A Damon Albarn A sexual encounter that happens after so much alcohol has been imbibed that, to be honest, the whole thing is a blur.

A Dollond & Aitchison Playing with yourself.

A Marianne Faithfull Sex involving a Mars bar.

A Marianne Unfaithful Sex involving someone else's Mars bar.

Bondage Getting tied up and having sex.

Bandage Getting tied up by a medical student and having sex.

Badinage Getting tied up in witty repartee so much that you forget you should be having sex.

The I'll Never Get Him Out Of My Room Shag Hey, look, you don't have to justify yourself to me – it was really late, you were really tired, you had that important lecture in the morning, and I'm sure he'll never tell anyone...

The Now Or Never Shag A type of end-of-term sex indulged in by people who've been pussyfooting around the issue for the previous ten weeks.

The Trophy Shag Sleeping with someone solely because of the kudos it gives to your otherwise dull and meaningless life.

The Atrophy Shag Sleeping with someone solely because you're petrified that if you don't have sex soon your bits will either drop off or dry up.

On the importance of insurance for university students

It is a sad reality that at university insurance is very important as every four minutes in the UK a student is burgled. And I can tell you she's getting very pissed off.

But seriously, given that crime both on and off campus is a major problem, you really should consider insuring your belongings. Especially as, for example, a £1500 laptop can be insured for as little as £75 worldwide, enabling you to sell it second hand, report that it was stolen, then claim back the full amount from the insurers – No, hold on a minute, that's fraud and is illegal. Forget I ever mentioned this.

There's always a better party going on somewhere else

Don't worry about it, it's a common feeling for every university student. And most of the time it's just not true. What's more, even if there is a better party going on somewhere else, all the people at it will be thinking just the same thing.

How to get to despise your really close friends in a remarkably short period of time

Move into a shared house with them.

Please turn over the corner of this page in case one of your parents picks up this book while visiting you.

Alcohol, though an integral part of university life, does have many drawbacks. If you must partake it's probably best to confine your drinking to the occasional weekend and never exceed one pint of beer or two small glasses of wine per day.

'Let's split the bills evenly'

When you first share a house a sense of fairness will probably suggest that household bills are divided equally. Unfortunately disputes inevitably will ensue because different people in the house use the facilities differently.

Some will forever be on the phone. Some will always be having their mates to stay from home so that every weekend the living room becomes an extra bedroom. And some (often called Dave) will insist on having the heating on full blast all the time even though it's actually June and not that cold.

So in no time you will be seething with resentment at having to subsidise someone else's lifestyle. Learning to cope with such bitter loathing is one of university's more useful lessons, as it stands you in good stead for your years ahead as a higher rate tax payer and as the parent of inarticulate, morose, ungrateful teenagers.

Six alternative ways of dividing up household bills

By usage.
By bedroom floor space.
By parental income.
By height.
By raffle ticket.
By moving out and leaving the others to pay.

Cooking for yourself

One of the major problems with university life is that your parents aren't there to cook for you. Hard on the heels of this shocking indictment of contemporary higher education will come the following realisations:

1. Mass-catered food, e.g. in halls of residences, is unlikely to place the people who award Michelin stars in any kind of dilemma.

2. Living off takeaways will rapidly deplete your meagre finances.

and

3. Cigarettes and alcohol – while the title of a decent early Oasis song – isn't, in strict nutritional terms, a balanced diet.

All of which means that you are faced with the undeniable and unpalatable (and I use that word advisedly) truth that at some point at university you are going to have to start cooking for yourself.

Now if that thought fills you with dread, don't worry. Everyone is nervous about the first time they cook. And while it may seem to be a vast and complex subject, with so many skills to master, in reality it's not.

Just so long as you accept the fact that everything you cook will taste like shite.

The only four recipes you'll ever need to survive as a university student

Soup   *Method*
              Fill a pan with tap water. Put bits of
              other stuff in. Boil.

Bolognaise *Method*
              Follow the recipe for soup except
              don't use water. Instead substitute the
              cheapest tin of tomatoes you can find.
              And add the cheapest mince you can
              get. For extra authenticity you can
              (apparently) add herbs. Boil.

Curry   *Method*
              Follow method for soup except use
              less water and add curry powder. Boil.

Ontoast   *Method*
              Put bread in toaster (or under grill).
              Turn on toaster (or grill). Wait. Remove
              toast. Put stuff on it. (Don't boil.)

The one recipe you, as a university student, should never ever try. Never. Ever

Ingredients   Half a teaspoon of salt. Three-quarters of a cup of flour. One cup of sugar. Three ounces of cooking chocolate. Half a teaspoon of baking powder. Three eggs. Half a cup of butter. Five grams of powdered hash.

Method   Melt the chocolate and butter together, then add the sugar, eggs and hash. Beat the mixture until creamy. Sift the flour, baking powder and salt together, and then add to mixture. Pour the mixture into a baking tin and bake for 30 minutes at 375°F. Remove, allow to cool, and cut into small squares. Eat. Giggle.

Sell by dates and use by dates

How seriously to take the dates emblazoned on the sides of packets of food really depends upon your attitude to risk. The cautious should probably try to consume the food within the same week. For the more bungee-jumping among you, anything above a month late will prove just how hardcore you really are.

Grunge, plunge and sponge

At the time of writing two styles of dress are favoured by female students for a night out. The first style is 'grunge'. This essentially involves dressing down in jeans, trainers, baggy tops, etc. The second style is 'plunge'. This involves dressing up with short skirts, clinging tops and plunging necklines.

(N.B. There is a third style called 'sponge' but this usually comes much later in the evening after too much alcohol has been thrown down and then thrown up.)

How, at university, to get a girl to think that you are a fascinating individual with a certain charm, an empathetic outlook on life, a great sense of humour, and the hint of sexual tension that makes you a definite possibility for a shag

It's easy. Ask her a question about herself. And try not to look bored when she answers.

How, at university, to get a boy to think that you are a fascinating individual with a certain charm, an empathetic outlook on life, a great sense of humour, and the hint of sexual tension that makes you a definite possibility for a relationship

It's easy. Ask them a question about football. And try not to look too bored when they answer.

Why it's only common sense not to work hard at university

It's all a matter of long-term self-respect. The logic of the argument goes like this. Say that while at university you do work really hard. In fact, because you are a conscientious individual, and value the opportunity you have been afforded, you work as hard as you possibly can. And then, having slogged your guts out, you only get an average degree.

If that were to happen, then for the rest of your life you would have to live with the fact that, intellectually speaking, you're not that hot.

Surely given that such a course of events is a distinct and depressing possibility, it would be far better not to work hard at university, do badly, and be able to console yourself with the fact that you could have got a much better degree if only you'd knuckled down.

How you, as a student, see banks

As a source of cash.

How banks see you (as a student)

As a long-term source of cash.

Why textbooks cost so much

It's a sneaky psychological ploy to make you believe that the information contained within them is both important and valuable. Unfortunately it is neither. It's just expensive.

The students are revolting

As a student it is vital, at some point, to be involved with a cause. Intellectually, psychologically and emotionally a cause can be a truly profound way of encouraging self-development and helping create a definition and an identity that is at one time separate and distinct from that of your parents, your family, your childish past, your school, your university and the whole range of oppressive, conformist and so-out-of-date forces that comprise the powers that be in society today.

More important than all that, choose the right cause and you can have some great parties.

After all, what better way to encourage a feeling of camaraderie at a party than the knowledge that you aren't just getting out of your head for the sake of selfish hedonism, but doing it for the good of mankind? And who can deny the excitement of realising under such circumstances that a drunken shag can be justified as a defiant stand against the forces of oppression?

Types of causes to get involved with

Essentially there are three main categories:

1. For.
In this category you are in support of or 'for'
something, e.g. you could be 'for' peace or
freedom, or equal rights for gay gerbils.

2. Against.
In this category you oppose or are 'against'
something, e.g. you could be 'against' war or
oppression, or the denial of equal rights for gay
gerbils.

3. Save The.
In this category you wish to 'save' something,
e.g. you could want to 'save the' whale, or the
planet, or the ring pulls off beer cans because if
you collect 200 you get a free cool box (for your
gay gerbil).

Choose a 'for' cause and you mark yourself out as an optimist who fundamentally believes in the goodness of people and that if only we all work together we can make the world a better place.

Choose an 'against' cause and you mark yourself out as a confrontationalist troublemaker whose parents might as well start saving now to build up a decent (ideally index-linked) bail fund.

Choose a 'save the' cause and you mark yourself out as a future building society manager. That's because it's just a short step from sitting down in the middle of the high street during rush hour shouting 'Save The Outer Mongolian Langoustine!' to sitting down in the middle of a very small, very drab office on a rainy Wednesday afternoon and suggesting to someone not yet 21 that they start 'saving for a pension'.

Bernie Ecclestone, eat your heart out

It's very hard for university students to break into Formula One motor racing. Formula Shopping Trolley, however, is open to all comers. For a basic grand prix you need at least two shopping trolleys, two pushers, two drivers, and a course agreed in advance.

Campuses and parks make ideal tracks. However, for that added Monaco-stylee glamour, excitement and sense of the crowd pressing in on all sides, nothing beats a race along the pavements in the town centre on a busy Saturday afternoon.

The university scarf

Why? What is the point? Ostensibly it lets people know that you go to that particular university. But I would argue that:

    a. Nobody else cares.

    b. You already know you go to that university.

All of which leads me to conclude that people who buy university scarves, while outwardly quite bright (having got to university in the first place), are secretly quite dim and need a surreptitious reminder of which actual university they attend. Especially when it's cold.

    This theory is backed up by the observation that the people who buy university scarves also tend to buy sweatshirts with the university logo on it.

The fleeting glimpse of a god or goddess

Occasionally, on campus, or across a crowded bar, you will spot a fellow student so mind-numbingly gorgeous that all possibility of rational thought will flee from you like an elephant escaping from an abattoir.

And for the rest of your time at university you will, from time to time, console yourself with the idea that one day you will meet said student, strike up a conversation and discover that they find you just as desirable as you find them.

Well, far be it from me to piss on your parade, but life isn't like that. Sorry. You're better off buying a lottery ticket. At least you've got some chance of winning that.

The three stages of a student night out

Years of research among students has revealed that the typical night out can be broken down into three stages.

Stage One   Expectation

Stage Two   Excitement

Stage Three   Disappointment

It is, I know, a harsh analysis, but it is better that you know the truth now before you start thinking that everyone else is having a far better time than you. Because they're not.

However, if an endless round of nights out all ending in disappointment is too depressing to contemplate, let me let you in on The Secret Of Stage Four. This secret, if used wisely will magically make even the most wrist-slashing night out a whole lot better.

Stage Four   Toast

The One Great Conflict

There is more chance of harmony breaking out in Northern Ireland, the Middle East or between Rangers and Celtic fans than there is of solving The One Great Conflict of student life. I speak, of course, of the intractable shared-house problem of: Whose Turn Is It To Do The Washing Up?

Over countless years the finest minds of each generation have approached the battlefield, eyes bright with naive optimism, only to retire bloody, bruised and convinced of the utter stubborn unreasonableness of their fellow man.

And as the crusty frying pans, mouldy plates and festering cutlery totter in the sink like some madcap Tracey Emin installation, and rejected peace plans lie scattered on the floor like mouse droppings at your favourite takeaway, you will come to the conclusion that has sustained students down the ages.

You don't have to wash up after a bag of chips.

Why university lecturers are invariably dull

It's because the life story of a typical university lecturer goes like this:

They were born, they went to nursery, they went to primary school, they went to junior school, they went to secondary school, they went to university, they stayed at university. And that's it.

Kind of explains a lot, doesn't it?

Thought for today

When, precisely, does a lie-in turn into a coma?

The compilation tape/CD/minidisc

This is a compilation made pretty much exclusively by male students which they give to a female student in order to convince them that they are a fascinating, sensitive, passionate person with wide-ranging tastes who's interested in them on many levels, including the cultural one.

However, most female students, while being outwardly flattered by this ploy, actually understand its true meaning, i.e. 'He wants to shag me.'

File under foreplay for music nerds.

A brief note for female students sharing a house with male students

Stop whingeing on about 'putting the loo seat down'. I mean, it's not as if you put it up after you've finished.

A brief note for male students sharing a house with female students

Flushing the toilet is not the same as cleaning the toilet.

Student loans. If they're such a great idea why not make them retrospective?

Currently politicians believe that student loans are a great way to finance higher education. These are politicians, you remember, whose own higher education took place under a system of student grants. What's more, these are the same politicians who either subtly, or directly, point to falling standards in universities and suggest that today's degrees are nowhere near as hard to come by as those in their day.

Combine all these facts and you come to the realisation that people who got a free education are making you pay for yours and on top of that claiming that the qualification you run up debts to achieve is not worth as much as the one they got for nothing.

Now surely that can't be right.

But students, unfortunately, have very little political power. And to consider just how important political power is in the decision-making processes of politicians, let's just extend the student loan model a tad.

If loans are such a good way of funding students today, wouldn't it have been just as good a way of funding students in years gone by? And if higher education does, as the argument goes, enhance the earning capacity of today's graduates, won't it have done the same for those who left having had their education financed by grants?

And if both these things are the case, who could possibly object to making the financing by loan retrospective and getting all those who graduated under the old system to repay the cost of their education? After all, it can't be that difficult to work out how much money the state paid for them, then factor in a reasonable rate of interest to cover the intervening years. Then the government could take the substantial tax windfall such an equitable scheme would raise and reinvest it in the education system.

Now why on earth would any politician shy away from such an obviously sensible policy?

Different types of superiority you will encounter at university

It's sad but true that for some students university is a great place to exercise spurious superiority over you.

Your best policy is to rise above their snubs and sleights and dismiss them as shallow, insecure losers. Or join in and snub and sleight others.

Intellectual superiority: I'm cleverer than you. I know long words. I use them in everyday speech. Therefore I'm better than you.

Moral superiority: I'm a more moral person than you. I want Third World debt cancelled. An end to world poverty. And I never eat at McDonald's. Therefore I'm better than you.

Artistic superiority: I only like movies with subtitles. Therefore I'm better than you.

Social superiority: Of course money is a crass and hollow way to stratify a society, but then again I've got more than you so, let's be honest, I'm better than you.

Inverse social superiority: Of course money is a crass and hollow way to stratify a society, but then again I've got so much less than you that somehow, because of my struggle and my parents' sacrifices, I am in some deeply 'authentic' way, better than you.

Religious superiority: My God is more Goddy than your God. Therefore I'm better than you.

Alcoholic superiority: God, I drank sooooo much last night! Therefore I'm better than you.

Emotional superiority: I'm in touch with my feelings. I talk about them to my friends. Endlessly. You don't. You don't even have real friends. They're just people you drink with. Deep down you're emotionally crippled. You're just a great big schoolboy. Therefore I'm better than you. (And I don't know what I ever saw in you in the first place.)

Phoning your parents for money

Tactically, it is a very questionable idea to just call your parents when you want money. Work on the tried and trusted three-to-one ratio of social call to begging call and you stand a much better chance of being continually baled out of persistent cash-flow problems.

Isn't 'higher education' some kind of typographical errer?

Given that the education that most students receive at university is only useful at university, and that they have to pay excessive amounts for it, surely 'hire education' would be a far more accurate description?

Student poetry

Oh, yes, please. Nothing will bolster your image as an angst-ridden, misunderstood and, above all, deep human being more than writing poetry. After all, a fair slice of emotional suffering, and contemplation of said suffering, is a fundamental part of the university experience. So get back to your garret and get it down in writing.

> in case
> you're wondering
> if what you write is
> poetry
> just lay it out
> like this
> avoid upper case
> letters
> and only write
> late at night
> when you're
> alone

(Also always try to end the poem on the single word 'alone'.)

Why it's vital that you make friends with overseas students

It's a case of good manners. These people are visitors to our country and as such it is our responsibility to make them feel welcome. I mean, imagine if you were studying overseas, think how grateful you would be if someone made the effort and came up and talked to you, offered to show you round and helped you settle in. So that's what you should do for the people who come here to study.

And, if in the course of your Good Samaritan act you clock up invitations for holidays to all manner of fabulous places all over the world, well, that's just a bonus that never occurred to you as a possibility at the time. Honest.

Late essay excuses

These fall into three main categories:

1. Personal Crises, e.g. illness, imagined illness, depression, imagined depression, accommodation problems, financial problems, emotional problems and, of course, imagined emotional accommodation problems involving financial difficulties.

2. Family Crises, e.g. illness at home, parental marriage break-up, death of a relative, funeral of said dead relative, and the deeply worrying funeral of a relative not yet dead.

3. Global Crises, e.g. the collapse of capitalism, the greenhouse effect, worry over tectonic plate shift, the war on terrorism, or worldwide panic over the possible reformation of Steps.

Of course, the science students among you can also choose from a whole range of scientific reasons why their essay is late. It just takes the application of a bright mind to come up with something plausible. For example:

'Sorry my essay's late but as you know the universe is constantly expanding and when I sat down to write the essay I found I couldn't reach my desk.'

'Sorry my essay's late but I reckon that the question you set was in fact a placebo and so had no educational value and therefore had no effect on me whatsoever.'

And as for those among you studying philosophy, well, I don't know why you ever bother to pretend that you might do some work when you can legitimately bandy about phrases like:

'What is "late" anyway?'

'What does "fail" really mean?'

Or the phrase you'll find most useful when you eventually emerge into the world of work:

'Do you want fries with that?'

Masturbation

Everyone does it. Everyone. It is neither shameful nor sordid. Though it can be messy. And once again it is one of the fundamental facets of university life. It's just that most universities tend not to mention it in their prospectuses. Which is a shame as a university description that went 'Outstanding academic standards, vibrant social scene, fine sporting facilities, good place for a wank' would, I'm sure, generate a lot of interest.

Mental masturbation

If actual masturbation is a key part of student life that involves pleasuring yourself by vigorously (or gently) rubbing your bits, then mental masturbation is a key part of student life that involves pleasuring yourself by vigorously (or gently) rubbing your intellect.

The other key difference between these two forms of fun is that while the first is usually a solitary affair, the second is most definitely a group thing. You sit around with others in someone's room, under the trees or in a student bar and get your intellectual dangly bits out, flop 'em around for all to see and try to convince the group that yours are the biggest, the firmest, the best shaped, the most aesthetically pleasing or the most frequently exercised.

The actual subject matter you discuss could be anything from philosophy, to global politics, to personal politics, to religion, to art, to whether Dipsy or Laa-Laa was the hardest of the Teletubbies. All that really matters is that you enter into the discussion with a passion, don't let lack of knowledge prevent you from holding forth, and be mature enough to realise that fun though such sessions can be, they're no real substitute for developing a meaningful, long-term, one-to-one relationship with an idea that you could eventually settle down with.

A little-known fact about university librarians

Most of them are into bondage and watersports.

Other people's food

It's two in the morning. You've just rolled in from a party. You're starving. You open the fridge. And, joy of joys, there's food. But it's not yours.

So what do you do?

If you even consider such a scenario a dilemma then my work with you is far from over.

You eat the food. You eat all the food. Should your housemate confront you in the morning, deny all knowledge then blatantly shift the focus of the discussion by accusing *them* of eating *your* food. Should your housemate continue their accusations and you find your resolve weakening, inform them that you were either:

1. Teaching them a valuable lesson on the harsh realities of the dog-eat-dog world that awaits them beyond the sheltered groves of academe

or

2. Just tidying the fridge.

Then run away.

One thing you must always minimise when talking to fellow students

The amount of work you've done for a particular exam. The more important the exam, the less revision you should own up to having ploughed through. It's a Reverse Intellectual Machismo thing.

One thing you must always exaggerate when talking to fellow students

How much you had to drink the night before. And how pissed you ended up.

A relatively simple step that any government could take if it were really serious about the value of higher education and truly wanted university students to get better grades

Ban daytime TV.

The power of words

Never underestimate the power of words. Use the right words at university and use them correctly and your apparent intellect will soar and both your lecturers and fellow students will look at you with renewed respect. If you doubt the veracity of this wisdom just consider this singular exemplar.

When you didn't know the answer to a particular question at school the chances are you would have had a 'guess'. At university only the most callow of students would do anything so gauche. No, at university the canny individual, when confronted with a query of which they are temporarily unaware of the correct response to, constructs a 'hypothesis'.

What follows is a list of the other 72 key words whose judicious use you should master if you really want to do well at university. But be warned: use them sparingly. After all, no-one likes a smart arse.

ancillary	anomaly	archetype	ascribe
axiom	cognizant	consensus	corollary
corroborate	crux	definitive	delineate
dialectical	dichotomy	dictum	didactic
disparate	dogmatic	eclectic	empirical
endemic	ephemeral	epistemological	exemplar
exigency	explicate	exposition	facet
generic	germane	gestalt	implicit
infer	integral	intrinsic	juxtapose
manifest	manifold	orthodox	paradigm
paradox	peripheral	pivotal	postulate
pragmatic	precedent	premise	presuppose
putative	ramification	rationale	requisite
schism	specious	singular	stratify
subjective	substantiate	superfluous	supposition
surmise	synthesis	tacit	tangential
tangible	tenable	tenuous	transitory
underlying	veracity	vestige	zeitgeist

And below are five words you should really try to avoid in all academic work you submit:

kebab, pantyhose, chunder, yummy, front-bottom

The one STD you should do your utmost to avoid

An STD is a sexually transmitted disease. Unfortunately they are a quite common hazard of university life. After all, you live away from the prying eyes of parents, you have a ready-made 'boudoir' always at your disposal, and bonk-hungry members of the opposite (or indeed same) sex are as plentiful as kippers in a kipper shop.

No wonder the risks of infection are great.

While the judicious use of a condom can protect you from many of the health dangers that might arise from a bout of the old jiggery-pokery, there is one STD, with particularly disturbing symptoms and side effects, that even the most industrial strength of rubbers can't stop.

I speak, of course, of love.

Love is an especially debilitating disease that has laid low many a university student over the ages. The range of symptoms it causes is diverse and often contradictory. It can lead to elation or depression, hunger or loss of appetite, lethargy or over-activity, the abandonment of close friends or the embrace of others you previously wouldn't be seen dead with. On top of that, a bad case of love can deal a particularly hard blow to your studies, as despite the fact you often do very little when 'in love' (the medical description) it still seems to take up all your time. Love can also turn you into such a soppy, daydreaming, smell-the-flowers kind of drip that your friends run a mile whenever you hove into view, unwilling to put up with another second of you banging on about the 'wonderful' disease carrier who infected you.

What's worse than all this is that students 'in love' think they are happy. But how can you trust the judgement of anyone who's suddenly decided that 'Vindaloo' by Fat Les is a great song because that's the first tune they and their new paramour danced to at the student union disco?

You have been warned.

One of the real joys of sharing a house

Few delights can compare with the feelings of camaraderie engendered by having to remove other people's pubic hairs from the plug hole of the bath.

'Where does the soap powder go?'

Look, I know it's not a top priority but there will come a point when you really should wash your clothes. That point will be when your clothes are so alive with grunge that one bleary-eyed morning they pick themselves up off the floor, sidle over to you in an embarrassed fashion and whisper somewhat shamefacedly:

'Hey, you know, like, sorry to bother you, but I really need a wash.'

Why it really is a waste of time tidying your room

Because you're only going to make it messy again.

One of the real reasons why it's important to have friends at university

It's so that you can have someone to go and see when you're feeling depressed and sit morosely in their room until they too are as miserable as you.

Vegetarians at university. A brief guide

The common-or-garden vegetarian Doesn't eat meat. Generally easy-going. And can be fun. However, dress sense may be a tad dodgy.

The ones who eat fish They eat fish on account, obviously, of fish being a vegetable. Though they seem harmless, this basic flaw in their reasoning should lead you to view almost all the opinions they hold with suspicion.

The fundamentalist vegetarian (AKA the Tofu Taliban.) For these people, vegetarianism isn't really about salads. It's about power. And the abuse of power in an irreconcilably materialistic, paternalistic and essentially oppressive world. All of which means that suggesting you bring back a 'Filet o' Fish' for them when you go on a Big Mac run might not be the best way to cement your friendship.

The vagueatarian By far the drippiest breed of vegetarian. That's because though they definitely class themselves as vegetarians they are annoyingly vague about what they can eat. Hence having them round for a meal or going out with them to a restaurant is as much fun as a fart in a frog suit.

The vogueatarian Invariably female students who are vegetarians because it's fashionable. And because all those models in *Vogue* are. And who really 'you know, like, respect my body'. Which is why they drink small bottles of mineral water. But doesn't really explain why they smoke so much.

The Johnny Vegasatarian Invariably male. Invariably hairy. Invariably live mainly on lentils. And real ale. Unlikely to have a girlfriend. May well be studying geology.

Student politics

It's very easy to be cynical about student politics.
So I will.

Everyone running for office in student elections
will tell you that it's really important for students to
take an interest and vote – after all, it is 'your
union'. Unfortunately, it's not important, and once
elected you will soon discover that instead of
running 'your union' the people in office are
running 'their union'.

The problem is that those elected, while having
impressive-sounding titles, have no real power. And
when you think about it logically this has to be the
case as the positions change every year. So all the
elected can really do is oversee structures and
practices that are already in place and functioning
fairly well. Hence the only decisions that can be
made are fairly minor.

The result is that the majority of students aren't
interested in student politics as they don't see how

it affects them. And the people who run for office end up as just another clique.

Which, bizarrely, is why student politics is important. That's because it is a system whose flaws, irrelevancies and general powerlessness pretty accurately reflect how politics operates in the outside world.

There, I told you it was easy to be cynical.

Student politics. An alternative approach

If there are things you believe in and causes you want to fight for, don't even attempt to do it through the existing structures.

Find your own path to the waterfall.

Ethics

University is by far the best place to have them. And society as a whole accepts that university is the best place to have them. So make the most of your chance to have principles and get all that kind of stuff out of your system while you're young. As in later years ethics will only get in the way of you improving what will probably already be a fairly comfortable lifestyle.

Noticeboard fun

All over every university you will find noticeboards for the use of students. It takes but a little imagination to generate all manner of fun by making up fictitious notices. My own favourite ploy is to offer a room in a too good to be true sounding shared house, at an equally too good to be true price. Then, as your phone rings non-stop, quiz the callers on a plethora of personal issues, until they hang up in disgust.

Alternatively, instead of putting your own phone number on the notice, use a friend's.

Why the language used in lectures is often impenetrable

It's because despite all their supposed intellect, a lot of lecturers haven't figured out the link between education and communication.

On the inherent schizophrenia of university life

How can you be over-confident and insecure at the same time?

It's easy. You're a student. It goes with the territory. Get used to it.

On finding food under your bed

Every now and then, as you grope under your bed for a lost sock or renegade bra, you will come across remnants of food. It might be a half-eaten sandwich, the congealed remains of a Pot Noodle, or the dried-up crust of a pizza lying prostrate in its box.

At the start of term you will, naturally, chuck said food in the bin. By the end of it, when money is tight, you'll eat it. Gratefully. What's worse is that you won't just stop at looking under your bed. You'll soon be searching under the beds of your friends too.

Where you drink affects what it costs

At university bars, drinks can cost anything up to half as much as in a smart venue in the town. So do the sensible thing. Drink twice as much.

Where you drink affects what it costs. Again

If you are going out drinking with your mates, do most of your drinking at home first, then go out. It's much cheaper that way. Much cheaper still is to go round to your mate's house, drink their booze, then go out.

Oh, the joys of 'house meetings' in shared houses

House meetings are usually called when there's an 'issue' to be discussed. This probably sounds very grown up and sophisticated, but in reality the 'issues' debated are rarely along the lines of 'Global Warming' or 'Is light a wave or a particle?' Instead, what you'll find yourself 'debating' are topics like 'Who keeps eating my food?', 'I should pay less as I've got the smallest room,' and 'Some people in the house never do the washing up, Dave.'

And now I come to think about it, 'debate' is too civilised a word for the level of discourse that usually ensues. Think Jerry Springer but with fewer inhibitions and you'll begin to get a feel for the tone of these meetings.

Please turn over the corner of this page in case one of your parents picks up this book while visiting you.

A good night's sleep is vital if you are to get the most out of your time at university. Hence always try to be in bed by 10.30 at the latest.

University. The natural habitat of the tentative grope

If you're a boy, it's something you should practise. If you're a girl, it's something you should look out for. The technique is straightforward and fairly easy to master. You stand facing or alongside your partner and your hand slowly traverses the small of their back. Then, casually, it slips south like a crocodile silently submerging itself in a lake to catch an unwary gazelle.

Though girls too can employ this tactic they're likely to feel more at home with a slightly more demure approach. I speak, of course, of the age-old favourite and self-explanatory Affectionate Hair Ruffle That Morphs Into A Caress.

(Incidentally, ladies, the only hair that should be ruffled in this manoeuvre is the hair on the back of your partner's head. Ruffle and caress hair anywhere else and you'll be sending out a completely different message, you brazen hussy.)

Student decor

Be warned, it's a thin line between 'shabby chic' and squalor.

Throwing a party. The Rule Of Thirds

For any party to be deemed a success, the Rule Of Thirds needs to have been observed:

1. One third of the people you invited.

2. One third of the people you recognised.

3. One third of the people you have no idea about, and they're the ones who seemed to be drinking all the drink.

Post-rationalisation

An invaluable concept for every university student to master. It enables you to retrospectively justify all kinds of dubiousness. It will, for example, help you explain why your essay was late, was crap and was on entirely the wrong subject. Or why snogging your girl/boyfriend's best mate was, in fact, a way of strengthening your relationship. Or why 'Actually, Dad, failing my exams is a great way of getting me to focus academically.'

In short, post-rationalisation is a powerful tool. So use it sparingly.

A guide for novices to the basic styles of dancing available at student discos

There are many schools of thought strutting their stuff at a typical university disco-style event. And how you dance says quite a lot about you. Unfortunately, hardly any of what it says is flattering. What follows is but a brief run-through of the major dance paradigms currently holding sway.

The cool
The ultracool
The shuffle
The riffle shuffle
The handbag circle
The coat circle
The handbag and coat figure-of-eight circle
The spastic
The spastic colon (very painful to watch)
The strut
The pony
The pony and trap (a version of the spastic colon usually only attempted by cockneys)
The bus stop
The hitch-hike
The 'my parents bought me a car so I don't need to use buses or hitch-hike'
The jock
The jerk
The jerk off
The jerk off and wipe down
The scrum

The head nod
The head nod and
  occasional knee bend
The head nod, occasional
  knee bend and tentative
  arm wave
The epileptic (not actually
  a dance, but often
  mistaken for one)
The pogo
The Pingu
The air guitar
The air catarrh
The John Travolta
The sway
The bob
The weave
The topple

The sway, bob, weave and
  topple
The booty shake
The bump
The grind
The bump and grind
The bump 'n' grind
The shake 'n' vac
The salsa
The salsa!
The grab
The grope
The grind
The grab, grope and grind
The grab, grope, grind,
  SLAP! and apology
The W.T.H.G? (Where's
  That Hand Going?)

Try to master as many as possible before you leave
university.

How to read textbooks

One of the most important aspects of studying the textbooks that you've bought is highlighting. Every university student should really master the art of highlighting as an invaluable aid to study. Indeed, highlight really well and you probably won't need to study at all. Here are the main approaches:

Underlining: For stuff that's important.
Double underlining: For stuff that's really important.
Circling: For stuff that's really, really important.
Asterisking: For stuff that's so important you need to write a note about it in the margin.

Then, of course, there are the joys of marker pens. I myself favour the snooker ball hierarchy of importance:

Yellow: For stuff you should be familiar with.
Green: For stuff you should memorise.

134

Pink: For stuff that you should get tattooed on the inside of your eyelids.

Black: For stuff so goddamned vital you can't even bear to look at it.

When you've finished marking up your textbook, each page should look like the team from *Changing Rooms*, high on hallucinogenic drugs, have had their way with it.

As such it will prove totally useless for study purposes. But tear the pages out of the book and post them off to the Tate Modern in London and you stand a good chance of being entered for the Turner Prize for contemporary art.

The mystical magical hour of ultimate comprehension

Between 2am and 3am the meaning of the world will become crystal clear.

On photo booths

It is compulsory for all students at some point in their university career to pile into a photo booth with their nearest and dearest mates and have a 'comedy' picture taken.

This is so that many years in the future, when you inadvertently come across said snap, you can marvel at:

a. the dodginess of your hair
b. the fact that you've never been in touch with any of these once-so-close mates since the day you graduated.

The learning curve. University style

The learning curve is a well-established phenomenon. It seeks to map out how information is accumulated over time. It starts out on a gentle incline, steepens while most stuff is learned, then levels out.

Unfortunately for university students, such a curve really doesn't accurately describe how information is gleaned. For them the graph stays pretty flat for ages, then lifts off vertically as end-of-term exams approach.

Beyond the learning curve

In spite of the questionable efficacy of the student version of the learning curve, by some unfathomable process of osmosis most students leave university with more knowledge than when they first went. They also tend to labour under the misapprehension that what they've learned might actually be of some use to them in the outside world.

That's when they encounter the two aspects of the learning curve that educationalists rarely ever talk about, i.e. how the learning curve extends:

1. The Learning Curve
2. The Plateau Of All This Stuff I've Learned Is Completely Useless
3. The Sheer Vertical Drop Of Forgetting

Why every student house should have a shopping trolley in the front garden

A lot of people will see it as an eyesore. I see it more as an extremely inexpensive anti-burglar device. After all, what says 'penniless students live here, nothing worth nicking' more graphically than a shopping trolley slowly rusting in a weed-choked front garden?

A brief explanation as to why university lecturers dress so badly

It's so the next time you go home you realise that, relatively speaking, your parents are incredibly stylish people who wouldn't look out of place doing catwalk shows in Paris, Milan or the Lakeside Shopping Centre, Thurrock.

A short list of courses that most universities don't offer, but should really start thinking about

How to make a pint last all night
Techniques and methodologies for chiselling
cheese off a grill
Milling about aimlessly
Talking bollocks
Is self-pity the same as depression?
How to carry a passed-out friend
Places to hide the good drink when you find it
at a party

The half life of cheese

The scientists among you will know that radioactive materials have what is called a 'half life'. This is a set period of time over which said radioactive material will lose half of its radioactivity.

Cheese, similarly, if left in a student fridge, has a half life. The difference with cheese, however, is that instead of losing its radioactivity and becoming less dangerous it actually becomes more dangerous.

The following is a rough guide to the transmogrification of cheese. It applies to cheese, left unwrapped, in a fridge.

1-6 days   Cheese is edible. Untainted by doubt.

7-13 days   Cheese dries and hardens. Like love left untended through the cruel frosts of winter.

14-17 days   Spots occur on cheese. Slightly worrying spots. But not so worrying that you refrain from eating the cheese. However, on eating it you will freely admit that it 'tastes a bit funny'.

18-27 days Fur starts sprouting from the spots. Rather akin to the hairs protruding from the mole on the chin of a much-loved grandmother – only somewhat finer in texture. As fur is not a natural quality in cheese, severe pause for thought will be had before consuming. The dilemma will be solved by scraping off the furry bits and surreptitiously serving the dodgy outer cheese to your friends while keeping the relatively unaffected core of the cheese for yourself.

28 days -6 months When you open the fridge the fur on the cheese has grown to such an extent that it screams 'Turn the fucking light out!' at you from the corner of the fridge where it has, like a homeless person in an underpass, barricaded itself in using other foodstuffs as makeshift walls. Should you be foolish enough to tackle it, it will grab you by the throat, push you against the kitchen table and demand 'Are you looking at me?' in a tone that would even have given a youthful Robert De Niro pause for thought.

Best eaten grilled.

'I know, let's all get dressed up the same and go out drinking – it'll be a laugh!'

This is a questionable tactic usually practised by female students who decide that dressing up in an ultra-tarty fashion somehow loses the less savoury tartesque connotations if a whole gang does it together. In any such groupings there will usually be one or two ringleaders who go for it full on, don't care what other people think, get out of their heads and do, indeed, have a laugh. All the rest, on the other hand, will feel decidedly uncomfortable, acutely aware that they look like a sex-starved strumpet desperate to pull anyone. So they'll actually drink less than they would normally. And not really have that much fun.

But the pictures will look great.

An easy way to supplement your meagre student income

Frequent the toilets of a student bar late at night when a band has been playing. Select a particularly inebriated compatriot. Usher them conspiratorially into a cubicle. Then sell them a rewrapped Knorr stock cube as an especially potent batch of 'North Senegalese Black'.

The beauty of this endeavour is that the next day who's going to admit to having shelled out for a stock cube in the bogs? But, just to be on the safe side, only sell to people smaller than yourself.

Another relatively easy way to supplement your meagre student income

First make friends with lots of overseas students. Then contact the CIA via the American embassy in London and offer your services as a long-term sleeper spy on the verge of infiltrating a sinister cabal of foreign 'intellectuals'.

Americans love all that kind of bollocks.

Why vegetarians at university always look so unhealthy

It's because they don't eat meat.

The student traffic-cone thing

It is a little-known fact that all incumbent governments when planning their fiscal budget for the year allocate enough funds so that all students in full-time higher education can have their own traffic cone. That's because governments believe that all university students will at some point in their university career benefit from waking up in their room with a hangover and a traffic cone.

The actual benefit to the student has never been made explicit before. But in the interest of enlightenment I will explain the logic. It is all to do with the allegorical nature of waking up next to a physical reminder of the night before's excess. As such the inanimate traffic cone is a very tangible warning to the student to be wary of what they pick up under cover of darkness, when drunk, because they will have to deal with the ugly object the morning after.

Hence it is clear that the government funds the student traffic-cone scheme as a pre-emptive warning against the dangers of casual drunken sex.

A simple technique for ascertaining credentials of a science lecturer

The more baggy and shapeless the jumper, the more academic and conceptually high-powered the research. The corollary of this law is obvious:

Never trust information from a smartly dressed scientist.

Why taking your washing home is such a great idea

On the one hand it's easier than doing it yourself. On the other hand it's cheaper than doing it yourself. And on the third hand it lulls your mum into a false sense of mumsiness that despite the fact you look all grown up on the outside, you still, in some ways, need her to look after you.

And while that warm glow of 'Ahhh, you're still my little baby...' envelops your mum in gooey nostalgia, you have an open goal of an opportunity to tap her for a little extra cash.

The toasted sandwich maker as metaphor

At the time it will seem like a good idea. And in the shop and on the box it will look so sleek and clean, enticing you into a world filled with all manner of hot, delicious, culinary treats. But in reality all you'll ever cook in it are cheese toasties. And the problem with melted cheese is that it tends to leak grease. And grease is really a drag to clean out of the crooks and nannies of a toasted sandwich maker. And the problem with that is that grease's best mates are dust and grunge. So within five toastings what was once pristine is now furry and grungy and splattered with rancid cheese globules. Which, for some obscure reason, isn't the image they chose to feature on the box in the shop.

All of which makes it a perfect metaphor for your room/lover/life.

House-sharing tip

Budget for the fact that you'll never get the deposit back.

Please turn over
the corner of this page in
case one of your parents picks
up this book while visiting you.

Drugs Will Kill You. It is a proven fact that even the most innocent experiment with the softest of drugs inevitably leads to a life of sordid degradation in which you gladly sell the sore encrusted emaciated skeleton that is your body for a few quid to sleazy businessmen round the back of the railway station just to raise enough cash for your next fix of heroin.

Just Say No.

Six degrees of inebriation

How drunk you got the night before can be gauged by the degree of spin you subsequently experience.

1. **Head spin:** You wake up and your head is spinning.

2. **Room spin:** You wake up and the room is spinning.

3. **Room spin 2:** You wake up and the room is spinning. And it's not your room.

4. **World spin:** You wake up and the room is spinning, it's not your room, you don't recognise the person next to you, and when you finally find your clothes, remember how to get dressed, figure out how to get out of the place and make it into the outside world, it too is spinning and continues to do so well into the evening, especially when, for some bizarre reason, you

decide that a full-on kebab would be a good way to settle your stomach.

5. **Life spin:** You wake up with the sickening realisation that 25 years have gone by and you've just come out of the operating theatre where you've had a liver transplant. From George Best.

6. **Death spin:** You don't wake up.

Just a thought

In every student canteen or cafeteria, at practically every mealtime, you'll see an overseas student eating on their own.

Maybe you should sit down and talk to one of them.

When you think about it logically it really should work

After a particularly heavy night, the way to stop a room spinning is to note the direction in which it is revolving, then stand in the middle of the room and rotate your body in the opposite direction.

It's a line of reasoning that's well worth a shot

If the Gap Year is such a good idea then surely your parents couldn't object to the concept of the Gap Term?

Is this the truth about student debt?

One of the things university is supposed to get you to do is question the world around you. To see beyond the obvious and uncover deeper, hidden meanings. Well, for a bit of practice, let's try with that ever-popular student subject – debt.

Student debt, it is universally acknowledged, is a bad thing. Yet the vast majority of students end up in debt. By the time you leave you'll probably owe money to the government, the banks, the credit card companies and your parents.

The education you receive is, in contrast, universally acknowledged to be a good thing. However, once you leave university you'll probably never use any of what you've learned ever again.

So if what you're learning is, on the whole, useless, what's the point of university?

In fact, could it be argued that just about the only thing you learn at university that's of any use in the everyday outside world is how to handle being in debt? After all, most students are reasonable, law-abiding people who accept that their debts are their responsibility so they know they'll have to get jobs to pay them off.

Look at it this way and then perhaps it's in society's interest to encourage student debt because it actually leads to stability. And the banks and big businesses are happy because students leave university used to living a life where they constantly spend more money than they have.

So maybe student loans aren't really about finding a way of funding higher education, but instead are a way of acclimatising the student to being in debt. Hence student debts aren't really a problem, but the solution to the problem of getting individuals to conform in a consumer society. And maybe the 'education' students receive is just the sugar coating on the pill that they're inadvertently swallowing.

But all this is just idle conjecture. I mean, this couldn't really be what's going on, could it?

Another great way to encourage 'cheery discussion' in a shared student house

If you use the last of the loo roll, it's always a jolly jape not to replace it.

Why drinking games are, essentially, bollocks

Drinking games are usually played by students who drink a lot anyway. So, obviously, the drinking bit isn't the point of them as the people involved would drink a lot even if they weren't playing a 'game'. As for the 'game' bit, well, they're not exactly a complex intellectual challenge. I mean, it's not as if you're sitting around playing chess or Scrabble and have to sink the remains of your pint if you can't think of a six-letter word starting with 'm' that has an 'x' in it. So the 'game' bit of the whole malarkey can't be the point either.

No, the whole point of drinking games is to annoy the other people in the bar. And to give rugby players a spurious sense of shallow camaraderie. Now in the main I'm all in favour of people annoying each other. But anything that makes rugby players feel good about themselves really should be discouraged.

The politics of parties

Never admit to having only one party to go to on a Saturday night.

'Welcome to the Barbie doll brigade'

Essentially it's a state of mind. It's a state of mind that says, 'I am strong, I am a woman and I have every right to go out looking like a finalist in the hooker of the year competition if I want to.' It's about rebelling against your parents, it's about celebrating a sexuality that you're becoming increasingly confident with, and it's about asserting your individuality in a world where so many people conform to boring norms. And, though you may only admit this to yourself, it's often about getting the bloke you fancy to fancy you.

Yes, there's a lot to be said for occasionally dressing like a tart at university. Acting like a tart, however, is a whole different kettle of kippers.

How many kidneys do you really need?

There are always means for a penniless student to raise some extra cash. It just takes a little imagination.

For example, there's a perennial shortage of healthy kidneys for transplant. You, as a young university student, have two. And unless you've had a serious drinking problem for some time they'll probably be relatively healthy.

Now conventional wisdom has it that you can only donate your kidneys after you're dead. Well, altruistic though such a gesture most definitely is, where's the benefit for you? However if, for an appropriate rental fee, you leased one kidney out while you're still alive, you're not only helping save someone's life but also earning some much-needed income for yourself.

What's more, as the sad truth is that the recipients of donated kidneys tend to be older and hence have a limited life expectancy, you'll be able to get the kidney back when they pop their clogs.

So you donate the kidney while you don't need it and get it back well in time for your later years.

And as the recipient of the kidney is unlikely to spend their final years drinking heavily, the kidney you get back will probably be in a lot better state than it would be if it had stayed with you.

It's a classic win-win situation.

I'm sure such lateral thinking is what the government had in mind when they switched student funding from grants to loans.

Why, scientifically speaking, chocolate is better than studying

Just consider the following two lists of ailments that commonly afflict students.

Things that can be cured by chocolate:
Depression
Stress
Broken heart
Lack of energy
Lack of chocolate

Things that can't be cured by studying:
Depression
Stress
Broken heart
Lack of energy
Lack of chocolate

Now I may not be au fait with the finer points of scientific method but I'd call that conclusive evidence that in the grand scheme of things chocolate is way more important than studying.

A three-part guide for improving the appearance of the typical student house

1. Remove all the light bulbs.
2. Perfect the art of getting up, getting dressed and leaving the house without ever opening your eyes.
3. Only return after dark. Preferably when drunk.

Personal tutors. Another interpretation

If you're unsure about how to think about your personal tutor, recast the relationship into one defined by the motor force behind contemporary Western society. I speak, of course, of consumerism.

Take this angle and it's easy to re-brand your personal tutor as a kind of educational personal shopper. Their job, as such, is to present you with a selection of intellectual ideas and concepts that they think might suit you. Consequently your job is to decide whether you want to buy what's being offered.

(My only word of warning is be wary of how much you buy, as the costs can soon build up, and most of what you get offered will only end up gathering dust shoved down the back of your intellectual wardrobe.)

A sad fact about all university gigs and discos

At a certain point in the evening a group of rugby players will form a scrum in the middle of the dance floor. I believe it's some form of primitive courtship ritual.

It rarely works.

'Mum, Dad, meet *(insert name of unsuitable student partner here)*'

Primarily a technique to be practised by female students. The gist of it is that at some point in your university career you bring home the most anaemic, hollow-eyed, drug-addled loser you can find and introduce them as your new beau.

The benefits of such a ploy are twofold.

First, you give your aged parents complete nightmares about the unsavoury life of debauched depravity said beau will be leading you into. (What fun.)

Second, and this is the real point of the ploy, everyone else you bring home in future will look like an adorable little cherub in comparison.

On wasting a whole morning doing nothing just because the sun is shining

This is a complete misuse of the word 'wasting'.

Why studying for an hour in the library never gives you an hour's worth of study

So you set aside an hour to study. In principle it all sounds very worthy. In practice it's completely useless. That's because a typical library study hour can be broken down as follows:

1. Arriving.
2. Finding the desk you want.
3. Finding the book you want.
4. Finding a friend in your sight line.
5. Nodding a 'hello' to said friend.
6. Realising that just a nod may be interpreted as a tad unfriendly.
7. Rescuing the situation by going over for a chat.
8. Returning to your desk and setting up all your stuff.
9. Opening the book and attempting to read the first paragraph.
10. Attempting to read the first paragraph again to see if it makes any more sense the second time around.

11. Deciding on a coffee break.
12. Recruitment of friend to accompany you on coffee break so that you don't feel so guilty about going.
13. The coffee break itself.
14. The return to your desk.
15. The realisation that a visit to the loo would be sensible before you get seriously stuck into your studies.
16. The visit to the loo.
17. The return to your desk.
18. The checking of your watch.
19. The shocking realisation that you've actually been hard at it for well over an hour.
20. Packing your bags and leaving. After all, there's no point in overdoing it. Or ruining your eyesight.

Another excellent library technique

Gather an intimidatingly large pile of books.
Surround yourself with them. Then, shielded from
prying eyes, read a magazine or text your mates.

Another house-sharing tip

Never have your name on the phone bill.

The top five 'girl power' anthems

As female university students have become increasingly pro-active when it comes to having as much if not more fun than male students, what can only be described as 'girl power' anthems have become more and more a rallying call for female solidarity and empowerment.

To fully enjoy this ladette-powered phenomenon it is imperative that you learn the words to the following and, while draping your arms round your mates' shoulders, unleash your full lung power whenever they're played:

1. 'We Are Family' by Sister Sledge
2. 'I Will Survive' by Gloria Gaynor
3. 'I Touch Myself ' by The Divynyls
4. 'Girls Just Wanna Have Fun' by Cyndi Lauper
5. 'The Bell Jar ' by Sylvia Plath

Saved

In your time at university you will occasionally be approached by sincere individuals imbued with the spirit of revelation eager to direct you towards the path of righteousness that their one true faith provides. If you are at all sensible you will recoil from their evangelical zeal, stare at your feet, and mutter something incomprehensible about being late for a lecture, having to meet someone, or being a worshipper of Satan.

Correct that such a response no doubt is, I would suggest that a far more productive course of action would be that, while making your excuses, you also get details of the salvation being offered.

Not that I'm proposing that you ever join said church/fellowship/cult – just keep the information to hand. Then should you ever reach a set of circumstances in which your parents start wondering why you're doing so badly at university, start talking to them about these new 'friends' that you've made and how so much of what they say makes so much sense. Then drop in the fact that you're thinking about going away with them for a week-long spiritual retreat. And start smiling a lot. For no reason.

Believe me, your parents will be so spooked by the possibility of you being cultnapped that all concerns about your academic failings will fly out of the window.

Just how important is your degree grade?

Well, I'll let you be the judge of that by telling you just how long your degree grade matters. It matters for the interval of time between getting the grade and getting your first job. After that, no matter how long you live, hardly anyone will ask you what grade you got at university.

Five things you can sell off in order to raise money at the end of term

Your books.
Your CDs.
Your laptop.
Your body.
Someone else's body.

(N.B. The last option is not strictly legal.)

A lesson in relativity, university style

It's amazing how what seemed a very reasonable workload at the start of term can turn into an outrageous one in the last week when the full implications of your ongoing 'I'll do it next week' policy finally become apparent.

Five fish beginning with 'H' that all university students should really be familiar with

Halibut
Huss
Herring
Hake
Haddock

There's always one housemate and their partner who make too much noise when they bonk

Picture the scene. You and the rest of your housemates have just settled down to watch *Countdown*. Housemate 'A' heads upstairs with their partner. Then just as the programme gets particularly gripping, it starts.

First you hear the creaking bed. Then you hear the headboard on the wall. Then you hear the soft panting. Then you hear the rhythmic grunting. Then it's the tender repetitions of 'Yes, yes, yes'. Then it's 'Yes, Yes, Yes'. Then it's 'Oh God, Oh God, Oh God!' And finally you get 'Harder! Harder! Hardaaaaaaagggghhhhhhhh!'

Honestly, it's enough to put you right off your Pot Noodle.

There are five courses of action available for the unwilling audience:

1. Turn the volume on the TV up.
2. Turn the volume on the TV down.

182

3. Quickly scribble out ice-skating-style score cards to be held aloft on the performers' return.
4. Practise impressions of what you've heard, to be repeated whenever the performers' names come up in conversation.
5. Retire to your own room for a little 'private time' because despite all your laughter and ridicule you secretly found the whole thing not a little arousing.

The choice is yours.

The 'to do' list. The university student variation

As term draws to a close you will inevitably find that you have too much to do, and too little time in which to do it. The sensible among you will try to address the quandary by making a list of 'things to do'. This, supposedly, helps concentrate your attention and gives you an incentive to sort yourself out.

Unfortunately such lists rarely ever work.

The most likely course of events is that after writing your list you actually only get round to doing one or at most two things on it. Then you get distracted by something far more pressing like drinking, carousing, navel-fluff sorting or an afternoon showing of a particularly implausible episode of *Murder She Wrote*.

Subsequent to this, every time you look at your list of 'things to do' you will become increasingly discouraged as it won't be getting any shorter but the time left to complete the listed tasks will.

Depression is but a mouse's footstep away.

That's why the canny student eschews the restricting confines of the 'things to do' list and opts for the sunny uplands of the 'things not to do' list. This consists of things that, in your opinion, it is a complete priority that you don't do.

A sample 'things not to do' list might include the following:

1. Don't take library books back.
2. Don't sort out holiday job.
3. Don't do washing up.
4. Don't start war in Middle East.

Now with a list like this even just a cursory glance at it once a day will leave you feeling far more positive about your achievements.

How to save money on food when living out

Make lots of friends. Then visit them, in rotation, at meal times. This is a particularly fruitful approach with overseas students. This is because they won't be sure that this isn't just a well-accepted British custom. Also they almost always come from societies where hospitality is a highly regarded virtue. And they always, always have the best food to be found anywhere at university.

Always wash whites and coloureds separately.

Why do you think they call university courses academic?

Because once you leave university they are.
Completely.

Another thing no-one tells you about university before you get there

A lot of the time it's really boring.

About The Author
(And Why You Should Buy
More Of His Books)

Hey, he's a really nice guy. Really nice. And on top of all that he's getting away with this writing mullarkey. He doesn't work very hard, but he makes a living. And he makes a living making people laugh. Now how fab is that? The problem is he's paranoid that at any minute someone official looking is going to turn up and shout 'Oi, you! Get a proper job.' And the thing is he wants to avoid that day as long as possible. And that's where you can help. If you buy lots of his books, and give them as gifts to your friends, relatives and absolute strangers you pass in the street there's an outside chance he'll never ever have to get a proper job again. Which, on the whole, is a good thing for all concerned as you really wouldn't want him driving any bus you were travelling on, or coming round to fix your toilet.

Growing Old Disgracefully is great to give to your parents. *The Parent's Survival Handbook* or *The Autobiography Of A One Year Old* are great for anyone who's got small kids. The little books on *Stress, Wrong Shui* and *The Kama Sutra* only cost a few quid and so you could even afford to give them to people you don't really like. And *The Book Of Christmas Stress* makes the perfect Christmas present. The best book, however, is *The Stocking Filler.* But unfortunately that's out of print.

All Ebury titles are available in good bookshops or via mail order

TO ORDER (please tick)

The Little Book of Stress	£2.50	❏
The Little Book of Wrong Shui	£2.50	❏
Stress for Success	£2.50	❏
The Little Book of The Kama Sutra	£2.50	❏
Autobiography of a One Year Old	£5.99	❏
The Parent's Survival Handbook	£3.99	❏
Growing Old Disgracefully	£4.99	❏
Christmas Stress (published Nov '03)	£4.99	❏

PAYMENT MAY BE MADE USING ACCESS, VISA, MASTERCARD, DINERS CLUB, SWITCH AND AMEX OR CHEQUE, EUROCHEQUE AND POSTAL ORDER (STERLING ONLY)

CARD NUMBER: ....

EXPIRY DATE: .... SWITCH ISSUE NO: ....

SIGNATURE: ....

PLASE ALLOW £2.50 FOR POST AND PACKAGING FOR THE FIRST BOOK AND £1.00 THEREAFTER

ORDER TOTAL: £   (INC P&P)

ALL ORDERS TO:

EBURY PRESS, BOOKS BY POST, TBS LIMITED, COLCHESTER ROAD, FRATING GREEN, COLCHESTER, ESSEX CO7 7DW, UK

TELEHONE: 01206 256 000
FAX: 01206 255 914

NAME:

ADDRESS:

Please allow 28 days for delivery.
❏ Please tick box if you do not wish to receive any additional information
Prices and availability subject to change without notice.